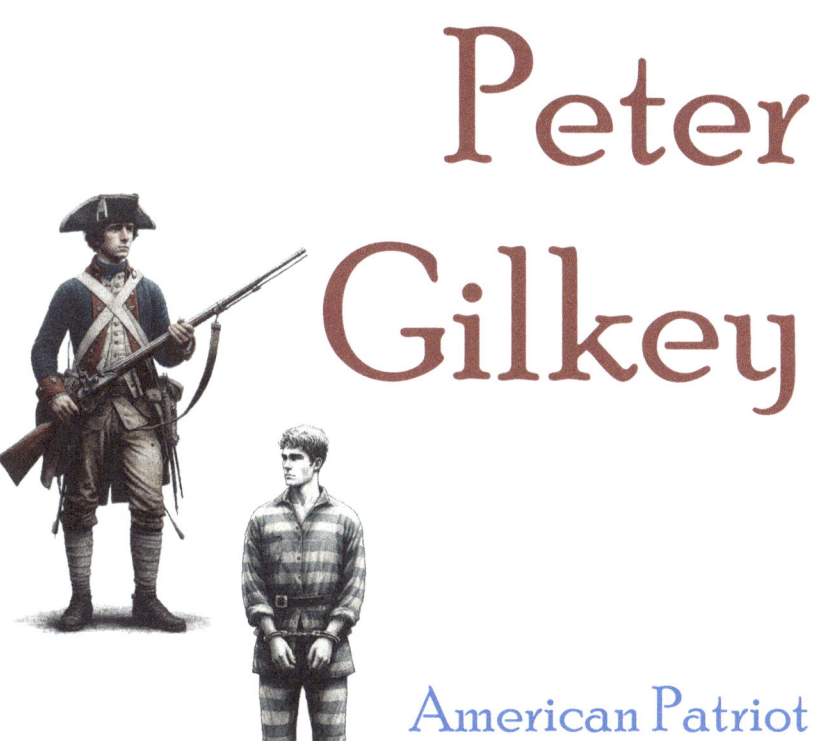

Peter Gilkey

American Patriot & Counterfeiter

John R. Guevin

Biographical Publishing Company
Prospect, Connecticut

Peter Gilkey

American Patriot & Counterfeiter

First Edition

Published by:

    Biographical Publishing Company
    95 Sycamore Drive
    Prospect, CT 06712-1493
    Phone: 203-758-3661   Fax: 253-793-2618
    E-mail: biopub@aol.com

All rights are reserved. No part of this book may be reproduced or transmitted in any form or by any means, electronic or mechanical, including photocopying, recording, or by any information storage or retrieval system without the written permission of the author, except for the inclusion of brief quotations in a review.

Copyright © 2024 John R. Guevin
Illustrations: CoPilot or as noted
Photo credits: as noted

              Publisher's Cataloging-in-Publication Data
Guevin, John R.
Peter Gilkey: American Patriot & Counterfeiter / by John R. Guevin.
1st ed.—Paperback
POD-I
ISBN-10: 1736901966
ISBN-13: 9781736901960
1. Title. 2. Prospect, Connecticut - History. 3. Cheshire, Connecticut - History. 4. Waterbury, Connecticut - History. 5. Connecticut - History. 6. Prospect, Connecticut - Anecdotes.
Dewey Decimal Classification: 974 United States History, Northeast
BISAC Subjects:
   HIS036030   HISTORY / United States / Revolutionary Period
   BIO006000   BIOGRAPHY & AUTOBIOGRAPHY / Historical
   HIS036100   HISTORY / United States / State & Local / New England
Library of Congress Control Number: 2024943563

Table of Contents

ONE	Introduction	5
TWO	Life in 1749: A Glimpse into a Young Boy's World in Northern Ireland	9
THREE	A Perilous Journey to America	13
FOUR	Life in Milford, Connecticut, circa 1750	19
FIVE	The American Patriot	24
SIX	Life in Transition	28
SEVEN	The Counterfeiter	35
EIGHT	The Hunter and the Hunted	38
NINE	The Trial	43
TEN	Visions of New-Gate Prison	46
ELEVEN	Gaol at Hartford Reality	53
TWELVE	Gilkey Family Released from Prison	59
THIRTEEN	In Search of the Gilkey Place	63
FOURTEEN	Conclusions	70
Chronology		75
Appendix		77
Bibliography		85

Acknowledgments

Appreciation is extended to the following people who provided significant assistance in the research for this book.

Carol Brooks, Prospect Historical Society, President
Dorothy (Dottie) A. DeBisschop, Connecticut Heritage
John Wiehn, Prospect Library, Director
Frances Martin, The Max R. Traurig Library and Archive, Archivist
Michelle Lisowski, Prospect Town Clerk
Patricia King, Cheshire Town Clerk
Morgan Bengel, Old New-Gate Prison & Copper Mine, Museum Administrator
Charles S. Miller, Waterbury historian

The author never had the opportunity to meet Charles S. Miller since he died the year of the author's birth. His manuscript, *Peter Gilkey: A Connecticut Counterfeiter*, was a critical part of this book. His son, Raymond H. Miller, presented his father's manuscript to the Prospect Historical Society in 1952. He also contributed to a detailed article about Peter Gilkey written by Lyall H. Hill in the Waterbury Sunday Republican in 1954.

For more information about Prospect, Connecticut, the reader is invited to contact the Prospect Historical Society. This organization collects and preserves the artifacts of Prospect and related materials; these collections are used for furnishing historic buildings, exhibitions, educational programs, and related activities for the benefit of all. The society encourages an appreciation of the history of Prospect and the preservation of the historic character of the town.

ONE

Introduction

Who was Peter Gilkey? If random people in his hometown were asked that question, the most likely responses would be, "Who?" or, "Oh, the counterfeiter." The author hopes that this book will help to answer the "who" question for the first group. As for the second group, they may come away with a more complete understanding of Peter Gilkey. He was far more than just a counterfeiter. He was actually only a counterfeiter for a small fraction of his lifetime.

Where Did He Live?
And just what was his hometown? Five towns in Connecticut could rightly lay claim to him: Milford, Wallingford, Cheshire, Waterbury, and Prospect. As a boy, Milford was the place where his family settled upon arriving in America. As a young man he made his mark in

Wallingford which then became Cheshire. A few years later, he became infamous in Waterbury. After his death, Prospect was incorporated. It absorbed the parts of Wallingford, Cheshire, and Waterbury where Peter Gilkey spent a good portion of his life. So Prospect can now claim him for all time.

Truth or Fiction?
Readers of this book may wonder if this is history or fiction. Some of the details seem hard to believe. But it is a true story. Truth can be stranger than fiction.

How Was This Book Compiled?
Wherever possible, original primary records were examined. That would include land, court, birth, marriage, and death records. These became the benchmark for weighing other information gathered. If details about Peter Gilkey's life can not be documented, the reader will be told.

One of the primary source materials was a manuscript titled *Peter Gilkey: A Connecticut Counterfeiter*. This work began to be compiled over a century ago. Charles S. Miller (1859-1943) was the author. He was a historian who lived in the East Farms section of Waterbury. Besides exploring Waterbury history, Mr. Miller had a keen interest in the history of Prospect. In particular, he had a special interest in the life of Peter Gilkey.

Oral Tradition
Miller obtained much of the information about Peter Gilkey from James Porter (1818-1906). Porter was born the year Gilkey died, so he did not know him. But Porter lived in Waterbury (now Prospect) while growing up with his grandmother Tyler on a farm next to the Gilkey place. The grandmother knew all about Gilkey firsthand. So it was passed down as oral tradition until Miller wrote the manuscript. To verify the information, Miller researched and documented everything using the Waterbury and Cheshire Land/Highway Records and the Court Records of New Haven.

Miller Pocket Diary
Another key resource was the pocket diary recorded by Charles S. Miller. The entries include his daily activities and those of his family, friends, neighbors, and coworkers, along with the weather and significant local and national events. Charles had a blacksmith and carriage making shop, and ran his own farm. He faithfully kept this daily record from 1876-1943— for 67 years. The last entry was the day before he died.

Beyond the mundane entries, there are many that have historical significance. His passion was history, and he knew a lot about Prospect and the people here. He visited the Hotchkiss, Cowdell, Clark, and many other families on a regular basis. His idea of fun was to talk about history and visit cellar holes and old homes. He seemed to know every home site in Prospect, past and present (at that time). Miller frequently took friends to see the Gilkey place after he was shown where it was in 1908.

Of interest, Nellie Cowdell of Prospect was his typist in the 1930s. She would type up his manuscripts, books, and letters. She may have worked on his Gilkey manuscript. In one diary entry, he noted that he paid Nellie $1.00 for some typing but overpaid her 25 cents! Farmers were frugal in those days. In 1940, he visited the Hotchkiss family and talked with them about their interest in starting a historical society. That group was later incorporated in 1945.

There was an entry in 1911 when he shared all he knew about Peter Gilkey with Mrs. Noble. He later wrote about reading a paper detailing the life of Gilkey to Ralph Pierpont in 1940.

The Prospect Historical Society Carries on the Tradition
An article in the Naugatuck Daily News on November 3, 1952, discussed how Raymond H. Miller, son of Charles Miller, visited the Prospect Historical Society. He gave a presentation about Peter Gilkey reading from his father's manuscript. From that time forward, it was traditional that members in Prospect would retell this story to

groups. Member Ed Fowler was one that took a particular interest in talking about Peter Gilkey.

Genealogical Research
Significant progress has been made in recent decades toward researching the genealogy of Peter Gilkey's family. Previously, only the middle part of his life was known. Now there is a more complete picture available. There is now a beginning, and there is an end. More work will certainly be done in the future to add to the understanding of this historic figure.

Book Organization
This book is basically in chronological order. To make it easier and more enjoyable to read, supportive documents are not included in the main chapters. An appendix is available in the back that contains historical records for those who want to explore those in more detail. There is also a bibliography that provides sources used in the research process.

Looking for Clues
The author invites readers to look for clues throughout this book that may help them answer some questions. A good history book will provide the facts about what, when, where, and who. My hope is that the reader will be able to better understand the *why*. Why did Peter Gilkey do what he did? Readers may also want to look for the people who were everyday heroes in this drama. Some may be obvious, others not so much. Finally, think about the victims. Were there victims? Who were they? The author's intention is not to answer all of these questions. That will be left to the readers.

TWO

Life in 1749: A Glimpse into a Young Boy's World in Northern Ireland

In the year 1749, amidst the rolling green hills of Northern Ireland, a young boy named Peter lived in a small village where everyone knew each other's names. At the tender age of four, Peter's world was simple yet full of adventure.

Family and Home Life
Peter was the son of a cobbler, Peter Gilkey, Sr., who was born in 1725. He was a man of modest means but rich in skill and reputation. Peter's mother was named Susanna. She was also born in 1725. She gave birth to Peter Gilkey, Jr., in 1745. [He will be referred to simply as Peter Gilkey going forward in this book.]

Most likely, their home was a humble stone cottage with a thatched

Typical Irish stone cottage circa 1745.

roof, nestled at the edge of the village. It had a single room that served multiple purposes: a workshop for his father, a kitchen, and a sleeping area for the family. The hearth was the heart of the home, providing warmth and a place to cook their meals, which often consisted of potatoes, bread, and the occasional fish or game.

Chores and Responsibilities
Even at four, Peter had his share of chores. He woke at dawn to the crow of the rooster, helped his mother fetch water from the welland gathered eggs from the hens. His small hands were perfect for weeding the vegetable patch and feeding scraps to the pig that they fattened for winter.

Schooling and Play
Education was a luxury that few could afford, and Peter's schooling was informal. It consisted of lessons from his mother in reading the Bible and basic arithmetic. His father taught him the names of the tools in the workshop, which planted the seeds of a cobbler trade he one day would inherit. Playtime was a burst of imagination with stick swords and stone castles and games of tag among the haystacks with the other village children.

Religious Life
Religious life was most likely woven into their daily routine. The religion of the Gilkey family is unknown. In Northern Ireland the prominent religion was Roman Catholic. Many attended the small parish church every Sunday without fail. Children learned prayers at their mother's knee, and families gave thanks before each meal. The church was also a social hub, a place where news was shared, and the community came together in both celebration and sorrow. Religion played a significant role in the villagers' lives. A parish church served as the spiritual center and a place for communal gatherings.

In 1745 a church and a cobbler shop were featured in almost all villages in Northern Ireland.

Occupations and Daily Life
Most villagers were subsistence farmers, growing what they could and raising animals like pigs and chickens. Any surplus produce or goods would be sold at the nearest market, which could be a few miles away. Being close to the sea, fishing would also be a significant part of their livelihood. Fish and shellfish sometimes supplemented their diet of potatoes and root vegetables.

Village Structure
The village would likely be divided into smaller sections, perhaps with names like Lower and Upper, indicating their position relative to the landscape. A village in Northern Ireland during the mid-18th century was a close-knit community where each family played a role in the village's daily life. The landlord of the area would be a prominent figure, and the villagers would rent their land from this person, sometimes subletting smaller parcels to others.

In 1749, a young boy like Peter would have experienced a life that was both challenging and enriching. His days were filled with simple pleasures, like the love of his family. His life was connected to the land and the community. It was a life that shaped him, as it did all those who lived in those times, into a person he would become.

THREE

A Perilous Journey to America

Moving to America?
The decision for a family to leave Northern Ireland for America in 1750, such as the family of young Peter, could have been influenced by several compelling factors:

Religious Conflicts
Many Irish families faced religious persecution and conflicts, especially if they were Catholic in a predominantly Protestant region. The promise of greater religious freedom in America was a strong influence.

Lack of Political Autonomy
Ireland in the 18th century was under English rule. This often meant that families had little control over their political destiny. Emigration

offered a chance for greater self-determination and participation in the governance of their new communities.

Dire Economic Conditions
Economic hardship was a common motivator for emigration. High rents, poor harvests, and limited opportunities drove families to seek a better life elsewhere. America, with its promise of land ownership and potential for prosperity, was particularly attractive.

Opportunity for Land Ownership
Land ownership was a significant incentive. In America, land was more accessible, and owning property was associated with wealth and status—a stark contrast to the situation in Ireland, where land was often controlled by a few. Many people were tenant farmers. This may prove to be the biggest motivator for why the Gilkey family came to America.

Better Prospects
The New World was perceived as a place of opportunity, where hard work and skill could lead to a better standard of living. For a cobbler like Peter's father, the growing towns and cities in America offered a chance to establish a successful business.

These factors combined to create a powerful motivation for families to brave the uncertain journey across the Atlantic in search of a new beginning in America.

And so at some point around 1750, the Gilkey family made the decision to leave their life in Northern Ireland behind and travel to America and start a new life.

The Ship
The ship that carried young Peter and his family from Northern Ireland to Connecticut in 1750 would have been a wooden sailing vessel designed for the transatlantic crossing. These ships were typically merchant ships that had been converted to carry passengers. They

were known for their sturdy construction to withstand the harsh conditions of travel on the ocean.

An example of a wooden sailing vessel circa 1750.

The ships varied in size but were often cramped, with limited space for passengers and their belongings. They were built with tall masts and multiple sails, allowing them to harness the wind effectively. Passenger numbers could range from a few dozen to more than a hundred, depending on the ship's size. Most ships leaving Ireland in the mid-1700s departed from Belfast or Dublin. Common arrival ports were New York and Boston for those heading for the Northeast.

Life Onboard
We do not know the name of the ship that took Peter and his family to America. Most likely, it would have been similar to other passenger ships of the era. Passengers like Peter's family would have been housed in the 'tween decks'—the space between the main deck and the cargo hold. The ships were equipped with lifeboats, but safety measures were minimal compared to modern standards. Navigation relied on the sun and stars; the captain and crew used sextants and compasses to chart their course.

Voyage Experience
The daily routine was dictated by the weather and the need to maintain the ship. Passengers would assist with tasks like manning the pumps or keeping watch. Entertainment was scarce. Passengers found ways to amuse themselves through storytelling, singing, or simple games.

The Dangers
The sea was a treacherous place in the 18th century. Travelers like Peter and his family faced numerous perils. Violent storms could toss their wooden ship like a toy in the waves. Diseases were rampant. Cramped and unsanitary conditions lead to outbreaks of scurvy which was caused by a lack of vitamin C. There was also the constant threat of piracy, and the wooden vessels were at risk of fire or running aground on unseen shoals. Misery was the most common description of a journey that typically lasted seven weeks.

The Food
Provisions on board were basic and monotonous. Peter's family likely subsisted on salted beef or pork, hard cheese, and ship biscuits, which were tough crackers that could last the duration of the voyage. Fresh water was scarce and often contaminated. The food was far from the comforts of home, and the lack of fresh produce meant that passengers, especially young ones like Peter, were at risk of malnutrition and disease.

Where They Slept
The sleeping arrangements were cramped and uncomfortable. Peter and his family would have slept in hammocks slung across the lower decks of the ship. These hammocks swayed with the motion of the sea, which could be soothing for some but nauseating for others. Privacy was nonexistent. The close quarters meant that everyone shared in the smells and sounds of shipboard life.

Duration of the Journey
The journey from Ireland to America could take anywhere from six to

There was little privacy in the living quarters on a 1750 sailing vessel with hammocks for sleeping.

ten weeks, depending on the weather conditions. For Peter, this would have felt like eternity, with each day blending into the next and little change in routine or scenery.

The Cost
The fare for a voyage varied, but it could range from £3 to £96. This was a considerable sum for a family in the 1750s. Many families had to work for years to save enough for the journey. Some passengers traveled as indentured servants, working for a period after arrival to pay off the cost of their passage.

Peter's journey was arduous and fraught with danger, but it was also an adventure that would lead to a new life in America. The courage and resilience shown by him and his family were qualities that would serve them well as they established their home in Connecticut.

FOUR

Life in Milford, Connecticut, circa 1750

In the mid-18th century, Peter and his family embarked on a life-altering journey from the rolling green hills of Northern Ireland to the promising shores of America. The year was around 1750, and it is believed the family settled in the town of Milford, Connecticut. Peter's father, a skilled cobbler, sought to ply his trade in a land where opportunity seemed boundless compared to the modest means they left behind.

The Gilkey family came to America nearly a century before the Irish Potato Famine, also known as the Great Hunger, which began in 1845 and lasted until 1852. The dire conditions in Ireland during and after the famine prompted a massive wave of immigration to America. But in 1750, there were relatively few immigrants from Northern Ireland. Finding others around them bearing the Gilkey name would have been very rare.

Most likely the Gilkey family rented rather than owned their home. There were no land records associated with the Gilkey name in Milford or other parts of the New Haven area at that time. Also, if they were Catholic, there were no Catholic churches in Connecticut, which was considered a mission territory. It can be inferred from records that the Catholic population in Connecticut in 1750 would have been very small, likely only a handful of individuals or families. If they ever saw a priest or attended a Mass, it would not be on a regular basis. Churches were often the places where records of births, marriages,

Depiction of downtown Milford, Connecticut circa 1750. Gencraft

and deaths were recorded. So for the Gilkeys, there were no such records.

A New Beginning in Milford

Upon arriving in America, Peter's family was in a very different world. The landscape of Milford was untamed, with dense forests and wide-open spaces that dwarfed their previous surroundings. The community was a melting pot of cultures and beliefs, a stark contrast to the unity of their village back home.

Peter's father could be quickly established as a cobbler, a trade in high demand in the growing town. Their home, while still modest, was different from their Irish cottage. It was likely made of wood, the most readily available material, with a simple design that reflected the practicality of frontier life.

For Peter, life in Milford was a blend of old and new. He learned local English, which became the language of his new life, while still holding onto the Gaelic words of his childhood. His playtime often involved exploring the surrounding nature, a vast playground that seemed endless compared to the familiar fields of Ireland.

Difficulties in Their New Life

In Connecticut, during the mid-18th century, Peter and his family would have faced many challenges as they adjusted to their new life. The New England climate was harsher and more variable than what they were accustomed to in Northern Ireland. Winters were longer and colder, which would have made survival and comfort a significant challenge, especially for a family of modest means.

While English was spoken in both Northern Ireland and Connecticut, there were still cultural and language barriers. The English spoken in America had begun to diverge from its European roots, and local customs and social norms would have been different, requiring adaptation.

As a cobbler, Peter's father would have had to establish his business from scratch in a competitive environment. The family would have needed to secure tools, materials, and a customer base, all while managing the financial strains of starting anew.

Acquiring land and establishing a homestead would have been a complex process. The Gilkey family had to navigate the legal system of property ownership, which was still developing and could be quite different from what they knew in Ireland.

Educational opportunities for children like Peter were limited. Often, Catholics were not admitted into the Protestant-dominated schools.

His Mother's Role

Peter's mother, like many women of the 18th century, would have played a crucial role in the family's assimilation and survival in their new environment. Women in the colonial era were often the backbone of the household, managing domestic affairs. Peter's mother would have adapted her skills to the new world, learning to work with local materials and altering her cooking and clothing-making techniques to suit the available resources. She likely sought out other immigrant families, perhaps even from their homeland, to build a sense of community. While her husband worked as a cobbler, Peter's mother may have contributed economically by taking in sewing or laundry, selling homemade goods, or even assisting in the cobbling business. Women's work, though often undervalued, was essential to the family's income.

Peter's mother would have played a significant role in his education, teaching him basic literacy and arithmetic, as well as imparting moral and religious values. She would have also preserved their Irish culture through stories, songs, and traditions. Mothers ensured that religious practices continued at home, perhaps covertly if necessary, to maintain their identity.

Conclusion

As Peter grew older, he would adapt to his American life. Milford may have been a brief stopping point and will not be the final destination for the Gilkeys. Records indicate that Peter will relocate again—this time to the part of Wallingford called New Cheshire, which will become Cheshire in 1780.

FIVE

The American Patriot

T his chapter is drawn from the manuscript of Charles S. Miller as detailed in the introduction. His words will be shown here and elsewhere in this book in italics. The first part is about Peter Gilkey's participation in the expedition against Spain in Cuba. The British were successful in this siege against Spanish-ruled Havana, which lasted from March to August 1762. The second part describes Gilkey's service in the War of the American Revolution in 1776. Between these two military events, Peter Gilkey will settle in New Cheshire, Connecticut.

Peter Gilkey was one of the one-thousand-man Regiment of Lieutenant Colonel Putnam sent by the Colony of Connecticut in 1762 in the expedition against Spain in Cuba. Havana was the principal object of attack. The fleet that carried the provincials sailed from New York and arrived safely off the coast of Cuba.

A terrible hurricane now arose, and the transport that bore Putnam and five hundred of his men was driven upon the craggy rocks and wrecked.

In this appalling situation, with the waves dashing against the ship with a force that threatened destruction, Putnam ordered every man who could wield an ax, saw, or hammer to make a raft of spars, planks, and other material that came to hand. Upon this raft, with the aid of paddles and wind, some of the men reached the shore. After a few of the men had been safely disembarked, the raft was pulled back to the wreck by ropes that were lashed to it, and then those who had gained the shore sided in pulling their companions to the beach. Such was the caution exercised by the commander that, in this manner, not a man was lost despite the critical conditions. Almost defenseless, Putnam camped here. The troops had saved their arms, but their powder was nearly all wet. For several days, they camped here, within twenty-four miles of the enemy. When at last the storm abated, a convoy took them aboard and carried them to Havana.

The midsummer climate proved fatal to a large proportion of our Connecticut soldiers who went on this expedition. Of the thousand brave men who landed at Havana, their mission being the storming of Morro Castle and the reduction of the city with its shipping and military stores to the dominion of the British crown, only a mere handful ever returned to their homes and native soil. A few officers and an occasional straggling soldier wasted to a skeleton were the sole survivors of that fatal campaign in which victory and death went hand in hand.

Peter Gilkey was one of those shipwrecked soldiers. Although he later took part in the storming of the forts and capture of the city on August 13, 1762, he did not return to Connecticut until a later date and year. Somewhere and somehow on this expedition, he became familiar with the manufacture of Spanish milled dollars, and brought back dies, tools, and formulas to be used in their making.

Charles S. Miller

Moving to New Cheshire

After Peter Gilkey returned from the Cuban campaign about 1763, he took up residence in New Cheshire, the western part of Wallingford. He lived here while serving in the Revolutionary War.

Peter Gilkey's Revolutionary War Service

Peter Gilkey was a soldier in the War of the American Revolution from the near beginning. From the scanty records of that time, we learn that in June 1776, when every able-bodied man between the ages of sixteen and sixty on the west side of the Connecticut River in this state was called to New York to defend the west border. Gilkey was in the Battle of Long Island, the great retreat to New York of September 15, 1776, at the Battle of Harlem Heights the next day and then took part in the Battle of White Plains. In this campaign, he served in Captain Samuel Pecks Company, Colonel Douglas's Regiment, Fifth Battalion, and Wadsworth's Brigade. His term of service expired on December 25, 1776. Many who went from Connecticut and served in Douglas's Regiment either died of sickness caused by hardship or were killed in battle.

Charles S. Miller

Spanish Milled Dollars

The interest shown by Peter Gilkey in the manufacturing of Spanish milled dollars while in Cuba was significant. It was the first indication of the direction his life would head over the next two decades.

At this time, the currency used in Connecticut, like much of the American states, was a mix of various foreign currencies. The absence of a standardized national currency led to the circulation of multiple forms of money, each with its own value and acceptance.

Spanish Milled Dollar

The most prominent foreign currency in America was the Spanish dollar, also known as the piece of eight. This coin held significant value due to its silver content and was widely accepted in international trade. In Connecticut, as in other states, the Spanish dollar became a benchmark for value, with other currencies often being valued against it.

Other foreign coins, such as those from Portugal and France, were also circulated. These coins were assigned local currency values in pounds, shillings, and pence, which were distinct from British sterling. The diversity of currencies created confusion and hindered economic stability. It underscored the need for a unified national currency that could facilitate trade and provide economic cohesion among the states. The Coinage Act of 1792 established the U.S. dollar as the standard unit of money and created the United States Mint to produce and circulate coinage. The first U.S. coins were struck in 1793, and paper money followed in 1861.

SIX

Life in Transition

Peter Gilkey's military service has ended. He returned to his New Cheshire, Connecticut home. He most likely practiced the trade of his father, working as a cobbler. But he had something else on his mind. Like many immigrants to the United States, he saw America as the land of opportunity. He dreamed of a prosperous life. He believed that path involved the making of Spanish coins. But to achieve that goal, he needed to own property. The records do not indicate he owned any property at that time. So he must bide his time.

Records suggest that Peter's father is still with him in New Cheshire. There is also evidence that both of the Gilkey men petitioned for land in western Vermont and eastern New York. For reasons unknown, the Gilkeys remained in Connecticut.

Peter Gilkey's Life in New Cheshire
There may have been a reason that Peter Gilkey moved to New Cheshire. Milford, established in the early 17th century, was a well-developed town. It was a hub of activity. In contrast, New Cheshire, established later in the 18th century, was a more rural and agrarian community. But New Cheshire has one thing Gilkey may not have found in Milford—land parcels that were remote, spread far apart, and were relatively inexpensive. That may have been part of his plan.

In 1768, Peter Gilkey married. His wife's name was Susannah B. (sometimes spelled Susana), similar to his mother. She was born in 1746. Public records revealed no details about the wedding.

Property Owners at Last
Time passed. The year was 1780. It proved to be a pivot point. Peter's father died that year. It is not known if the father left any inheritance to Peter.

That same year, the town of Cheshire was incorporated. On May 19, 1780, the state legislature established Cheshire as a separate town. This day was called the Dark Day and was one of great drama. At midday, candles were lit in homes. Birds began to roost. Some of the legislators meeting in Hartford to consider Cheshire's petition for township declared that the "Day of Judgement" was at hand and wanted to adjourn, but Colonel Abraham Davenport of Stamford, who was at the session, saved the day. *I am against adjournment. The day of Judgment is either approaching, or it is not. If it is not, there is no cause for adjournment: If it is, I choose to be found doing my duty. I wish, therefore, that candles may be brought.* History of Cheshire

Colonel Davenport may not have been worried about the sudden darkness, but perhaps Peter Gilkey should have seen this as an omen not to do what he was planning to do.

Forty five days later, Peter and Susannah arrived at the First Congregational Church in Cheshire, that was built in 1694. That building served as the town hall for Cheshire. The town clerk opened the land records book number one to page eight and recorded the deed for the parcel.

The cost was £6, 3 shillings. The transaction was put in Susannah's name. It was rather unusual for a woman to purchase land at that time. But the clerk added "wife of Peter" after her name. The source of the money was noted as the incumbrance of the widow's dower. This referred to money set aside from her husband's estate in case she became a widow at some time. Typically, this was established at the time of the wedding. The land was described as a small slip of land of

The Gilkey's first house may have looked something like this.

seven rods (about 115 feet) with a dwelling on it. In today's language, it was a starter home. The seller of the parcel was Ashel Andrews, who was the administrator for the estate of the deceased Stephen Bunnel.

The Gilkeys were now land and home owners. They may have been the first in their line of Gilkeys (going back generations) to own land. It would appear that the fulfillment of Peter's plan had begun. But there was an unusual twist ahead.

An Early Case of Property Flipping?
About eight months later, on Feb. 25, 1781, Peter and Susannah were meeting again with the Cheshire Town Clerk. On that day, they sold the same parcel that they had recently purchased. The buyer was David Morgan (sometimes Morgin). Only this time, the sale price was £15. They netted a sizeable profit! The deed noted that improvements were made to the house and land. The Gilkeys were building their assets. Records suggest that Susannah may have been related to the Morgans in some way.

A Second Land Purchase
A little less than one year later, on February 12, 1782, Peter Gilkey purchased ten acres of land in Waterbury along the boundline highway (really just a narrow dirt road) adjoining Cheshire. That boundary between Waterbury and Cheshire was called the "Devil's Backbone" in a map from 1796. The frontage along the highway measured 44 rods (about 726 feet) and extended about 36.4 rods (600 feet) west of the highway. The seller was Ellas Hotchkiss of New Haven, who received £18. There was no house on this property.

Soon Peter Gilkey and his partners, Isaac Hine and Abraham Tyler (more about them later), built a house on the Waterbury property. Unusual details about this house emerged from the manuscript by Charles S. Miller.

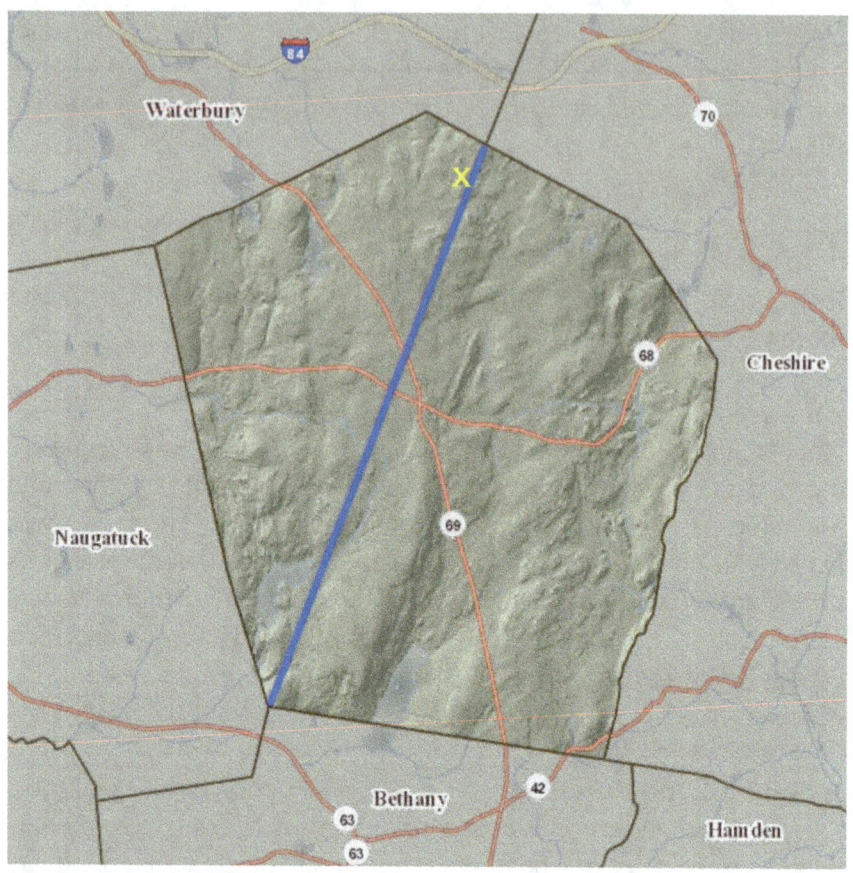

Modern map of Prospect showing the boundline highway in blue. The area to the west of the highway was Waterbury in 1782. The area to the east was Cheshire. The Gilkey property is indicated by a yellow X.

A Most Unusual House
The spot he built on was lonely, retired, and secluded, far from the traveled road. The nearest house seemed to have been that of Isaac Hine, located nearly a mile away to the southwest. All about was a wild forest, except for the boundline highway, which was but a mere path open to the public at that time. Three quarters of a mile south, where now stands the large grand house of Mr. George Cowdell, no building had been erected. The first close neighbor was Thomas

Benham, who built a dwelling house on land given by his father, John Benham of Cheshire, two years after Gilkey had left. Half a mile to the north, may be seen the ruins of an ancient cellar and chimney. Here Daniel Baldwin came from Wallingford in 1792 and bought land of Phileman Heaton and Silas Hine 10 years after Gilkey had. Here, he built his house and made a home.

After Gilkey's house was finished, he, Hine, and Tyler dug another cellar, smaller and below the first. This was fitted up as a shop, and was planned with consideration and care taken in covering it over that it should not be observed. Abraham (earlier spelled Abram) Tyler made the bellows and built the furnace; Gilkey furnished most of the tools. The metal was melted and mixed by Gilkey and cast in thin strips. These were hammered and flattened on an anvil to the proper thickness, then scraped bright, blanked on the anvil with a ring die and punch, then struck up with a rude drop they had made, and finally milled on a hand miller. So perfect was the imitation, that they had but little trouble in disposing of them through their agent in distant places or exchanging them for bills and lawful currency.
Charles S. Miller

Gilkey's Plan Becomes Reality
And so, the decades-old dream of Peter Gilkey was now a reality. He crossed the line from being an ordinary citizen, who made and repaired shoes and boots, to being a criminal—a counterfeiter. He must have known it was a crime. The elaborate scheme he devised, with all the secrecy, isolation, and deception, indicated he knew what he was doing. He did it anyway. But why?

Partners in Crime
The two partners that assisted Gilkey in his illegal operation both appeared to be upstanding members of the community. Abraham Tyler (1738-1823) served as a sergeant in the company of Capt. John Lewis in 1777. He also fought in the war in 1780. Years later, Abraham's son Lyman would write: *When 14 years of age, I ploughed the land, (rough it was and hard soil), and sowed rye and harvested it and*

planted corn and potatoes and worked the farm with only the help of brother David, age 12, while father Abraham was away in the army.

Isaac Hine (1743-1807) was a cousin of Ambrose Hine. He served as a captain in Col. Beardsley's Regiment of Militia, that fought in New Haven, Fairfield, Bedford, and Norwalk. He married Eunice Wilmot. Isaac's will of 1804 mentioned his children: Chloe, Freemen B. and Susanna. Isaac and Eunice were interred in the old Prospect burial grounds at the south end of the Prospect Green.

The Gilkey Children
Amidst all this activity, Susannah and Peter gave birth to a boy named Cary on October 31, 1782. They already had another boy named William, who was born about 1780 or shortly thereafter. The 1790 U.S. Census revealed that they would have five children at that time.

Cheshire Property Question
Who occupied the property the Gilkeys sold in Cheshire? David Morgan purchased the property. But did he live there? One possibility is that Morgan could have rented the house back to the Gilkeys after buying it. The Gilkeys needed a place to stay while they built the house in Waterbury. Confirming records have not surfaced.

There was a clue in Charles S. Miller's manuscript, which opened up the possibility that Gilkey (or his partners) may have occupied the house located in Cheshire.

It seems odd that at this time, there was some doubt as to the town that Gilkey belonged to. The writer has in his possession a writing that was given to him many years ago by a Cheshire man. The paper on which it is written is dark with age, and it reads as follows:
"This Certifies that Peter Gilkey, now resident in Waterbury, is an inhabitant of the town of Cheshire. November 25 A. D. 1782."
Charles S. Miller

SEVEN

The Counterfeiter

The manuscript by Charles S. Miller advanced the story. When necessary, clarifications are offered in brackets. All seemed to be going according to plan for the counterfeiting operation.

To find the location of the Gilkey place, go north on the Summit Road from Merriman's filling station at the crossing of the New Waterbury and Straitsville Roads till the square turn in the road to the east is met, then continue north on the old path, about half a mile, and the old cellar may be found about ten rods west of the old highway. There is a small run of water between the highway and the cellar. Here in 1781 and 1782, Gilkey, assisted by Isaac Hine, Abram Tyler and another (whose name was never learned), manufactured unknown quantities of Spanish milled dollars. After they were manufactured, they were buried in the ground for a length of time, taken

Making Spanish dollars in the hidden sub-basement at the Gilkey house.

up and placed in a hard leather bag, and shook till they had the appearance of having been used, then buried again for a short time.

The fourth member of the party was unknown to the local inhabitants, as he lived far off beyond New Haven, where he had access to New York. He visited the Gilkey place only at night, and never talked with anyone but Gilkey. He took quantities of the money, practically all, which he exchanged, bringing back Continental bills, "Lawful Money," and the base metals, which were melted, mixed, and made into money.

It was said that Gilkey never spent any of the money that he made. Although he was a shoemaker by trade, he never followed that vocation while living here; yet after they had been there a while, he seemed to have more money than it was usual for the men to have in his state and surroundings. This, together with a mysterious air about the premises, made people wonder where he got so much money.

* * *

All went well with Gilkey and his associates. They made their coins and prospered, yet as time went on, minor things happened that caused Gilkey to be suspected of counterfeiting. Tracks were seen where horses had been up and down the road at night, and lights were seen at a late hour about the place; an unusual event that was not clearly understood.

Charles S. Miller

The fourth member of the Gilkey partners in crime enterprise appears to have been William Perkins from Cheshire. Along with Abraham Tyler, he assisted Peter Gilkey in making the forge used in the operation. This was revealed in records at the Connecticut State Library:

Perkins, William, Cheshire, sentenced for making forge for Peter Gilkey & petition for liberty granted on giving a bond for good behavior & payment of costs, Oct. 1783 VI: 229, 230.

Tyler, Abraham, Waterbury, sentenced for assisting Peter Gilkey in making a forge. Liberty allowed on payment of costs & giving a £200 bond for good behavior, Oct.1783 VI: 231, 232
    CT Crimes and Misdemeanors Series 1 Index, pages 99, 102

EIGHT

The Hunter and the Hunted

Peter Gilkey's elaborate plan began to unravel, and it did so very quickly. The discovery of his counterfeit operation was primarily the result of the efforts of three people. One was a concerned citizen, a hunter, who saw something (or, in this case, heard something) and then said something. The second was a person with special needs, one with savant syndrome, who had perceptions above and beyond those of most people. Finally, there was a sheriff who had the courage to employ in his investigation a person with special needs because of his unique skills. So these three players in this real-life drama were the heroes. Without their contributions, Gilkey's illegal enterprise may have continued for much longer.

This portion of the Charles S. Miller manuscript described the discovery of the counterfeiting enterprise. Clarifications and portions changed with more appropriate language are offered in brackets.

However, in the fall of 1782, a man, who lived in the vicinity of what is now Prospect Center, went with his dog and gun up into the Muskingum Woods to hunt [raccoons]. *These woods lay north of the Gilkey place, and were divided by the boundline highway but stretched far to the west in unbroken forest. The name is said to have been of Indian origin. But how Muskingum came to be applied to this region is unknown, although the earliest records refer to this vast woodland by that name.*

These woods seem to have been bound on the north by the original Wallingford and Waterbury Road, which was the first road in this vicinity, and over it passed many of the first settlers of the eastern part of Waterbury—the Austins, the Beaches, the Johnsons, the Mixes, the Benhams, the Culvers, the Humistons, the Hoadleys and many others.

This road began in Wallingford and passed through the Notch-in-the-Rocks to continue northwest across the valley and up the steep mountain onto the present Plank Road near the residence of Mr. Frank A. Brooks. It continued across the Waterbury town line, a mile up from what is now known as Manthy Road. Here, it bordered Muskingum land for more than a mile.

At its highest point, the path became nearly straight, crossing the present Scott Road near the top of the first hill and onto the power plant of the Scoville Manufacturing Company, where it crossed the Beaver Pond Brook. (There is a new concrete bridge there now.) The road continued down the valley of the Beaver Pond Brook to the crossing of the Mad River, where history states, "that the first Mill Stones were brought over in 1680." This crossing was a little below the present Plank Road Bridge, and the path does cross the present Plank Road a little northeast of there. It also crossed Knoll Street, Englewood, and Idylwood Avenues, and the northeast corner Hamilton Park, where it united with Farmington Road (now East Main

Street) about twenty-five rods the present junction of Meriden Road.

But the hunter, who left his home near Prospect Center in the late evening and whose name cannot now be recalled, had hunted over a portion of the woods and started to return home with his dog some time after midnight. We were not told of the luck he had hunting, but as he was walking along the road, he heard a sound or thud that seemed to come from Gilkey's house, which was located some distance from the road and was perfectly dark. Having but little fear, for he bore the same flintlock musket that had served him through the [Revolutionary War], *he approached near the building and found that the sound definitely came from the house. He then went home.*

The next night, with a neighbor, he visited the place, and again they heard the heavy blows. The next day they reported their findings to a public officer. He suspected Gilkey of counterfeiting, so he went to the Gilkey place with a sheriff, a search warrant, and a posse of men. Among this posse was [a person who appeared to have savant syndrome. His name was not mentioned, but the author will call him Amias.] *At times, Amias astonished people by his acts. They retired to the place at midnight and found it all dark, but sounds were distinctly heard at regular, quick, short intervals. They knocked for admission, as the doors were heavily barred. The sound ceased, and soon they were admitted. A search was made, but nothing unusual was found. However, two men were up with the rest of the family in bed.*

The officers left the house reluctantly, knowing that some great mystery existed.

They had nearly all reached the road, and called Amias to hurry, as he had stopped by the brook. When he caught up, Amias said to the Sheriff, "What makes smoke come from the chimney when there is no fire in the fireplace?" Some thought there was a fire and favored going home. Finally, the Sheriff went back and saw the smoke.

The sheriff and his deputies confirm the smoke coming out of Gilkey's chimney, as pointed out by Amias.

They again entered the house, and were more thorough in their search, causing all to get up, but though they went through the bedding and looked everywhere, no metal, tools, or coins could be found to indicate that counterfeiting had been carried on there. The smoke could still be seen issuing from the chimney, although no fires could be found. Again, they were nearly ready to give up the search, when one jumped up and down on the cellar bottom and found that it was hollow below. Fresh earth was soon discovered under the stairs, beneath which a trap door was found leading down to a smaller sub-cellar, which was fitted up as a shop.

Gilkey claimed this to be a place where he did his mechanical jobbing. Here a small blast fire was burning, the draft of which was connected with the chimney of the house. The tools had been recently used, and the melted metal, the owner explained, was to be cast into bullets, a quantity of which was on hand to shoot foxes, wild cats, bears, and other wild animals that inhabited the nearby forest.

They found no evidence that money had been made and were ready to leave the place, when they called Amias, who observed the smoke coming from the chimney. He had remained in the cellar, and when he came up, Amias had half a die for making Spanish Milled Dollars that he had dug up in an inconspicuous place. This led to a further search, but no more evidence was found.

Gilkey claimed that no one could prove that he had ever spent any Spanish Milled Dollars. They arrested him, and he was taken before a Justice Court in Waterbury, and bound over to the Superior Court at New Haven.

Hine and Tyler were arrested soon after.

Charles S. Miller

NINE

The Trial

C harles S. Miller picked up the narration. The crime was planned and executed over a long period of time by Peter Gilkey. By comparison, justice in the state of Connecticut was very swift. As will be revealed in the next chapter, justice for the Gilkey family may not have been very fair—certainly not fair by our modern standards.

Gilkey was tried before the Superior Court at New Haven in February 1783 and sentenced to prison for two full years, and fined Thirty Pounds plus costs of suit—17 Pounds, 18 Shillings and 3 pence. His fines were payable to New Haven County.

* * *

About this time, Tyler and Hine were arrested, brought before the Waterbury Court, and charged with being accomplices. Each was fined about sixty pounds Lawful Money. With the costs included in their fines, however, their total fines amounted to about $300, a large sum in those days. They were both residents of the vicinity and considered men of means, yet it developed years after that they dug up some of the buried treasure, which was taken to New York State to be exchanged for Lawful money, in order to pay. They did not have to use many of their metal dollars, for at that time, one hard dollar was worth about sixty-three continental dollar bills.

Charles S. Miller

Treatment of Counterfeiters

The State of Connecticut was particularly harsh in its treatment of counterfeiters. Editor Dorothy A. DeBisschop in her book *Connecticut's Old Newgate Prison*, indicated that in 1770 counterfeiters could have their right ear cut off. They could also be branded on the forehead with the letter "C" by a hot iron, and whipped on the naked body, producing twenty stripes. If the counterfeiters were convicted and unable to pay these costs, the court was empowered to sell the convicted criminals as indentured servants, using the money received to cover the costs. The sale into indentured service would not be made until after the convicts had served six months in jail at hard labor. Peter Gilkey was fortunate that he was not apprehended a few years earlier.

Entire Gilkey Family Sent to Prison

As unbelievable as it may seem, Peter's wife and children were forced to go to prison along with him. Susannah, her infant son Cary, and her son William, about two years old, were placed in the same prison as Peter and the other inmates.

The State of Connecticut seized all of Peter Gilkey's land and assets as a partial payment for his counterfeiting crime conviction. This left him destitute and unable to support his family. So the state ruled that

Woman and children sharing space with inmates in Gaol at Hartford circa 1783.

the family had to join him in prison.

While it may seem unusual, the practice of family members joining a relative in prison was not entirely unheard of in the Colonial era. Prisons during this time were not exclusively places of punishment; they also served as a means to isolate individuals from society. The concept of incarceration as a form of punishment was still evolving, and the conditions within these facilities were far from the regulated environments expected today

TEN

Visions of New-Gate Prison

The words from the judge detailed below when he was found guilty must have been a shock to Peter Gilkey. The reputation of New-Gate Prison as a wretched place was widespread. It began as a prison for British loyalists during the Revolutionary War. Then it transitioned into a prison for common criminals. At that time, prisons and jails were designed to be a deterrent to crime. The theory was to punish rather than reform. New-Gate added an extra layer of discomfort from other prisons—the harsh, cold, and damp underground living quarters of a former copper mine.

"Sheriff or his Deputy, Greetings. Whereas Peter Gilkey of Waterbury in the County of New Haven, on the last Tuesday of February 1783, before the Superior Court held at New Haven, was found Guilty of making instruments for forging and Counterfeiting

Spanish Dollars, whereof said Court under Judgment against the said Peter that he be committed to the Common Gaol in Hartford, there to remain until the New-Gate Prison shall be repaired and fit to receive Prisoners and then be committed to New-Gate Prison."

County of New Haven Court Records

The manuscript of Charles S. Miller resumed with a description of what life would be like for Peter Gilkey at New-Gate Prison. The story that Mr. Miller provided is nearing its end. There was crime, and now there will be punishment—and it will be harsh.

How New-Gate Became a Prison

New-Gate Prison, where Peter Gilkey was [sentenced], was formerly a copper mine located in the north part of the town of Simsbury—now the town of Granby. Here, mining was carried on at times prior to the Revolutionary War but was entirely abandoned in 1772. The ore found here generally produced only 12 percent metal, so it was never very profitable to the owners and operators.

The State of Connecticut conceived the plan of using the mines and underground cavern for prison purposes. At this time, there were two shafts, one about 35 and the other 75 feet deep. They were not far apart, and at the bottom, they were connected by tunnels and levels. These tunnels were extended in several directions as they followed the different veins of copper—some a short distance, while others extended many feet into the mountain.

In 1773, the old mine was fitted as a prison by providing a ladder in the west shaft that extended to the bottom and a heavy oak and iron-strapped door at the top; it was secured by a huge hasp and padlock. Nothing was done with the east shaft, which was much deeper and had straight, smooth sides. The first prisoner put in was for stealing a horse, but he had only been there a few days when his lady friend went there at night with a long rope, which she lowered down the east shaft and soon pulled him up to liberty. The next year, several prisoners were admitted, but they all escaped. At that time, they worked mining copper, and they were kept underground nearly all the time. They used the tools furnished them to enlarge the drains and make openings, so they got out. In 1775, the east shaft was closed, a log guard house was built over the west and a work shop was erected above ground, together with a keeper's house. Soon, all the buildings were enclosed with a picket fence. Those renovations were finished in 1781, but the fence and buildings were set on fire and destroyed [in 1782].

For a time, the idea of maintaining a prison at this place seemed to have been abandoned. However, the several jails in the state were overflowing with prisoners. The legislature had now passed a bill providing not only for the repair of the old fixtures, but the building of larger workshops, keepers' house, guard houses, etc., all to be enclosed within a strong stone wall. . . .

The Daily Work for Convicts

At daybreak every morning, the heavy trap door covering the shaft was unlocked and lifted open by the united strength of two men. A guard of soldiers with loaded muskets stood in line before it. A bell was rung calling the convicts from the depths below to their daily toil. Slowly and painfully, they ascended the thirty-five-foot ladder and hobbled along the way to the workshop, followed by a guard, where they were placed at their work. Another squad followed in a like manner till all were up or accounted for. Some were chained with leg shackles to their anvil blocks. Others, by one wrist to wheelbarrows, and such as the vicious and refractory, had an iron collar suspended by long chains from beams overhead locked about their necks.

The guards took their stations. The hand cuffs and shackles were removed, and the labors of the day began. This consisted principally of blacksmith work. The prisoners made nails, hinges, hasps, and staples for doors; fireplace cranes, irons, and equipment; and later even wagons were made. Twice during the day, work was suspended for an hour of meals.

Meals
Pieces of salt pork or beef were distributed to each man, which were washed and boiled at the forges in the water provided for cooling the irons. One pound of bread, a few potatoes, some vegetables or apples, and a pint of cider made up the daily ration. Each one divided his ration for the day to suit himself, and they were allowed to trade with each other.

Sleeping
After a time, the number of prisoners increased, presenting the need for more sleeping accommodations. These were structures about eight feet high and a little less in width, with a shingled roof to keep the water that dripped from overhead off the sleepers. These structures were merely set down in the cavern, and provided two floors—one about a foot above the stone floor of the mine and the other about two feet higher up. On these floors, the prisoners lay on straw without covering. Much of the labor on these sheds was done by the prisoners.

Working for Pay
Regular tasks or stints were given to the men, and when these were finished, they could work for themselves. In this way, some of them acquired considerable sums of money. Some made ingenious trinkets and rude models from the copper which they melted out of the ore they dug in the night down below.

A Tavern Treat
Captain Viets, who had charge of the prison for a long time, lived and kept a tavern opposite the prison gate, where the prisoners were privileged to go and procure luxuries in the form of cakes, pies, cider, tobacco, liquors, and so forth, provided they had money and could prevail on some of the guards to escort them over and back again.

End of the Day
At four o'clock in the afternoon, the work of the day was finished.

The hand cuffs and shackles were replaced, the collars and fetters unlocked, and with a slow walk and a hobble, the men, unless granted the indulgence of remaining for overwork, made their way back to the pit. As they passed the trap, a bit of a candle, an inch long, was given to each. Holding up his shackles as best he could, each then backed slowly down the ladder to the regions below.

After a time, all were not cuffed and shackled when they were sent below. The faithful and trusted were not obliged to wear irons. But the unruly and vicious, and those who injured the weak, were heavily shackled and, in other ways, punished.

A Chapel and a Bakery
A chapel and bakery were erected at different times of brick and stone. A mill was also added for grinding meal and flour. The power for the mill was furnished by a huge treadmill about 10 or 12 feet in diameter with treads long enough for eight or nine convicts to step on side by side at the same time, each man having a small stall to tread in by himself. This wheel drove mill stones that ground the meal and flour that were used in making the bread and mush for the convicts.

Stewart—The Escape Artist
Among the prisoners . . . Stewart [William Stuart], *who had been arrested in Fairfield County for robbing and injuring a man, so he died later. This Stewart escaped from every prison he was put in. Finally, he was apprehended and taken to New-Gate for safekeeping.*

The prisoners were obliged at certain times to attend religious services in the chapel. At one of these services, the corpse of a prisoner, who had died the day before, lay in a rude coffin on a table near the door. After the service was over, the men filed out, and Stewart quickly, and unobserved, dodged back of the door. After all were gone, he took the corpse from the coffin, placed it back of the door, and got into the box himself.

After a time, two [men of color] *came and took the coffin to a hill some distance southwest of the prison and began digging to bury it. They soon heard a sound from the corpse, which made them wonder; so they started to investigate, albeit rather timidly, as they were frightened at the sound. As they were about to put their hands on the box, they heard a deep, solemn, bass voice exclaimed, "The dead will arise and come forth with the sword of Gideon." Now thoroughly frightened, one exclaimed, "He* [has] *a big sword!" Abandoning all*

From within the coffin, a deep, solemn bass voice exclaimed, "The dead will arise and come forth with the sword of Gideon." The grave diggers fled in fear. Stewart emerged from the coffin and fled, never to be captured again.

pretense of burying this corpse, they ran to the prison and told what they had heard. Stewart kicked the lid off the box, ran to the woods, and was never retaken.

Charles S. Miller

This story about the escape of the convict by taking the place of another convict who had died was confirmed by the staff of Old New-Gate Prison & Copper Mine. They were not aware of the prisoner's name (William Stuart) until the author informed them of what Charles S. Miller's manuscript revealed. Prisoner records of the Old New-Gate Prison confirmed that William Stuart was an inmate there. New-Gate had a reputation for being a site of numerous escapes. The prison's design included deep shafts and extensive tunnels from its days as a mine. This provided multiple opportunities for resourceful prisoners to escape.

Double Standard
Hypocrisy about counterfeiting was on full display even in the 1700s. The copper mine that later became New-Gate Prison had an operation on the site that made copper coins. At that time, there was a shortage of small coins, and this operation helped fill a void. But this was not a legal mint. It was just a private enterprise. The government looked the other way. So a place that punished counterfeiters was itself a counterfeiting operation. The prison eventually closed due to its inhumane conditions and the construction of a new state prison in Wethersfield.

Today, the Old New-Gate Prison & Copper Mine is a state-operated archaeological preserve and museum. It reopened to the public in 2018 after restoration and offered guided tours of the historic site, including the Colonial-era copper mine and the remains of the prison.

ELEVEN

Gaol at Hartford
Reality

Gilkey's visions of New-Gate Prison were put on hold. First, Peter had to deal with life at the Goal at Hartford, otherwise known as the Common Gaol or just Gaol. Gaol was an early British word for jail. The building was located on the corner of present-day Pearl Street and Trumbull Street. A serious fire at New-Gate forced the transfer of all inmates to other prisons and jails and delayed the arrival of new ones like Gilkey. The anticipated quick repairs at New-Gate never happened. The facility was inoperative until it re-opened in 1790.

Some historians recorded that Peter Gilkey served his prison time at New-Gate but that appeared not to be the case. Prison records at New-Gate do not list his name. Also, when he was finally released from confinement, it was the Keeper (warden) of the Gaol at Hartford that was directed to do so.

History of Hartford Jails

In 1641, Hartford opened its first jail on the north side of State Street (presently Market Street), where it served the county for almost 100 years. In the mid-18th century, Hartford leaders sold the "prison land," including the building and its contents, and moved the jail to the "highway" (now Pearl Street). In the decades that followed, Hartford

Depiction of Gaol at Hartford, circa 1783, which was located at the corner of Pearl Street and Trumbull Street. The exact details of the building are not known. But about 80 years later, the Hartford Jail at this same location was a larger, four-story structure.

ushered prisoners through a revolving system of different structures . . .

Crime and Punishment, Hartford, September 10, 2021
ConnecticutHistory.org

The Gaol at Hartford, unlike the subterranean confines of New-Gate, was designed as a prison. The living conditions at the Hartford Jail in 1783 were often deplorable, with overcrowding, poor sanitation, and inadequate food and medical care being the norm. Prisoners were subjected to a strict regime, with little to no concern for their welfare or human rights. Peter Gilkey's sentence, served at the Gaol at Hartford instead of the infamous New-Gate prison, might have offered a slightly less punishing experience, though it was by no means easy or humane.

The Common Gaol institutions were scattered across Connecticut, with notable ones located in Hartford and New Haven. They served as the primary detention centers for those who ran afoul of the law. The jails were typically situated in county seats, where they were accessible for the administration of justice. They were simple structures, sometimes just a part of the local courthouse, and were not designed for long-term confinement.

Inmate Life in Hartford Gaol
The cells were cramped and poorly ventilated, leading to unsanitary conditions that were ripe for the spread of disease. Inmates suffered from cold in the winter and oppressive heat in the summer. The diet was meager, usually consisting of bread and water, with occasional servings of meat or broth. Medical care was virtually nonexistent, and prisoners with health issues often had to rely on the charity of local physicians or the kindness of jailers.

Conditions for Gilkey's Family
The seizure of Gilkey's property and assets by the State of Connecticut left his family destitute, unable to fend for themselves. It was indicated earlier that Connecticut decreed that Gilkey's wife and

children were to accompany Peter Gilkey to prison.

The conditions that the Gilkey family faced in the Common Gaol at Hartford would likely have been dire. Prisons of the 18th century were overcrowded and unsanitary, with all prisoners—men, women, children, debtors, and those with mental illness—housed together, regardless of their crimes. The prison system was under development, with no national rules governing its operation. Wardens were unpaid, earning money by charging inmates for basic necessities.

For Gilkey's wife and children, life in prison would have been a struggle for survival. They would have been subjected to the same harsh conditions as the other inmates, with little to no provision for their welfare. The experience would have been traumatic, especially for the children, who would have been exposed to the adult prison population and the realities of criminal punishment at a very young age.

Justice in the 1780s
By modern standards, it seemed the justice system was inhumane in Gilkey's day. In many ways, it was. But there were some positive aspects. The grim life in jail probably kept many would-be criminals off the street and thereby protected the general public.

In 1783, the ability for inmates to appeal sentences and petition grievances was available. What was not readily accessible for poor prisoners was legal representation. Many defendants had no choice but to represent themselves in court. This approach was challenging. Court proceedings were complex, and prisoners lacked legal knowledge, which put them at a disadvantage. Some courts appointed lawyers to represent poor defendants. However, this practice was inconsistent and often depended on the judge's discretion. In other cases, local leaders, religious figures, or concerned citizens advocated on behalf of the accused. It is not known how Peter Gilkey obtained legal representation, but he did. The appendix lists appeals that Gilkey submitted while incarcerated and afterwards. Some of these petitions were granted and others were not.

Here are excerpts from his first petition through his legal representative:

... he freely confesseth with Shame & remorse before Your Honors, that he was reduced to this wicked scheme & was about to put it into Execution but never in fact did do ... that your Honor^g would be satisfied with the forfeiture of his Estate & the Imprisonment he hath suffered hitherto & solomly promises never more to offend. He hath a wife & children now with him in Prison, ... they are destitute & distrest and have nothing—the memorialist is also wounded in one of his hands and fears it will be lost intirely ... he most Earnestly begs your Honors Graciously to forgive the remainder of his Imprisonment & suffer him to go home with his poor Family & begin the world anew & live in Peace with all men ... Dated at the Gaol, May 1783.

Peter Gilkey followed up the petition with a letter later in 1783 to a person unknown. This may be the only example available where Gilkey spoke directly in his own words:

Hartford, October 8, 1783
Sir: You are Not unacquainted with the Circumstances of my being Confin'd in Hartford Goal. Should be very glad you would do your utmost to Procure me Liberation from this place by putting in a Petition to the General Assembly at their present Sesion that I may be discharged, but if this Request be not Granted I shall be glad you would put in a Petition to have me Removed to New Haven Gaol as it will be more Convenient on many accounts as being nearer my friends and family and the transportation of the Necessary articles of Life will be far less expensive and as my Family are under indigent Circumstances I shall be glad you would afford your assistance for their and my Relief and you shall be amply rewarded for your trouble by your very obliging friend and Servt

Peter Gilkey

The petitions were eventually granted. Gilkey was released in 1784 after serving less than his full two-year sentence. The exact date is unknown.
Resolved by this Assembly that the said Peter Gilkey be discharged

from any further Imprisonment in Virtue of said Conviction, and the Keeper of the Gaol at Hartford is hereby to liberate the said Gilkey accordingly.

Having achieved success and gaining an early release, Peter Gilkey made another petition. This time he sought to have his fine reduced or forgiven:

. . . that your Honors have Graciously pleased to remit a part of the Imprisonment . . . that while he was in Jail he most unfortunately, by an accident (had) a wound in his left hand & wrist, so that he hath almost wholly lost the intire use of it—that he hath a wife & children to support, one of his children being very weakly & never likely to recover . . . That his small house & Ten acres of indifferent Land is all he has in the world and this has been taken from him to satisfy the afore^{sd} Fine and Cost—The Memlst earnestly entreats Your Honors Mercifully to forgive him the said Fine & he will struggle to secure the Cost . . . A. Dom.1784

This time, the Assembly refused to forgive the fine. Peter Gilkey and his family would never occupy their former home again.

Many other prisoners made petitions. Most of them voiced concerns they had about the conditions of their confinement, such as lack of heat, poor light, terrible food, crowded cells, and shortages of clothing and bedding. While these grievances were no doubt warranted, they involved the prisoners personal comfort. The petitions Peter Gilkey made were largely focused on the welfare of his family. He placed his family first.

TWELVE

Gilkey Family Released from Prison

*P*eter Gilkey petitioned the Legislator for release and a restoration of estate. He was wounded and could not work, and his family was suffering from destitution, and he would pay costs, fines, and so forth within six months.

His petition was heard, and he was discharged from prison. He hoped for restoration of his estate and returned to his old home in Waterbury (now Prospect). But in his absence, all was changed. The walls of the cellar and chimney were ruined, the ground about had been dug up, and other great damage had been done by curious people who had been looking for treasures. Gilkey stayed about the place for a few days and then disappeared—no one knew where. After a time, he returned to Cheshire, and paid up his obligations to the state. He never pressed his claim for restoration of his estate. Instead, he went to East Farms in Waterbury and bought property [for a home and leased another property for 995 years with a shoemaker's shop on it to work again as a cobbler].

* * *

At the time the above purchases were made, some people were mystified as to how he had so much money. It was revealed long afterwards that, while he was at his old place, he took the secreted dollars away and exchanged them for Lawful Money.

Here, Peter Gilkey lived with his family for about five years, pursuing his old trade of shoemaking and repairing boots and shoes. After a time, he sold out and moved to Cheshire. The shoemaker's shop he leased to Elijah Sperry for 989 years for six Pounds Lawful Money, and the house he sold to Abraham (also spelled Abram) Tyler, who was the father of Elijah Sperry's wife.

Elijah Sperry was from Hamden, and was a blacksmith by trade. He had served long in the army, and was one who helped forge the great chain that stretched across the Hudson River at West Point in the Revolution. He intended to make the shoemaker's shop into a blacksmith shop. But on the petition of Capt. Phineas Castle, Joseph Beach, and others, the town took it over and turned it into a school house. Mr. Sperry bought land on the west side of Farmington Road, nearly opposite his home, and built a blacksmith shop there. After a few years, Sperry sold out and moved to Vermont.

The land in Prospect, which Peter Gilkey bought and on which he built the house where the counterfeit money was made—the same land that the State of Connecticut took over for debt in 1783—remained the state's property for about thirty-six years, when it was purchased by Elisha Platt.

* * *

The above is the last record we have concerning Peter Gilkey. During the thirty or more years we have known him, his life was fraught with danger, hardship, and crime. He lived through the years when rational events "tried men's souls." From whence he came and whither he went, we know not.

Charles S. Miller

Mr. Miller may have exhausted his supply of records, but newly revealed information sheds light on the final years of Peter Gilkey. First, he appeared in the 1790 U.S. Census. That was the first census ever taken. It indicated that Peter Gilkey was living in Cheshire. His wife

Burying Ground Hill, also known as Grand Street Cemetery, in Waterbury as it appeared in 1891. This was where Peter Gilkey, his father, and Susannah Gilkey were laid to rest. Soon after this photo was taken, the Silas Bronson Library and Library Park were constructed at this site.

Photo: Mattatuck Historical Society

was still with him, and he had five children. There were four sons under the age of 16 and one daughter.

We also learned he died in 1818 at the age of 72 or 73. He had purchased a burial plot at the cemetery on Burying Ground Hill, which served Waterbury from 1695-1890. He was buried there, as was his father in 1780. His wife, Susannah, was also buried there, although it is not known when she died. As for Peter Gilkey's mother, there is no record of her death or burial. Some of the headstones from that first cemetery were relocated to the wall around Library Park in Waterbury. This was done at the suggestion of various patriotic organizations in 1934.

Burying Ground Hill Cemetery Memorial at Library Park, Waterbury, Connecticut.   Photo: Find a Grave

THIRTEEN

In Search of the Gilkey Place

When Peter Gilkey was sent to prison and the State of Connecticut seized his property, there was a surge of fortune seekers that stormed his property with shovels and pickaxes. They were looking for Spanish dollars that might still be hidden somewhere on the property. If any were successful, the property raiders weren't talking. That raised an interesting question. Is it any less of a crime to have stolen counterfeit coins and spend them like real money than to make the coins in the first place? The reader can make that judgment.

Finding the Gilkey Place
Those early coin seekers had no trouble finding the place. Everyone in the area knew about Gilkey's crime and where his property was located. It was also only a short distance off the boundline highway,

which was as easy to travel as other roads at the time.

Within a year, they had thoroughly trashed the place. When Peter Gilkey returned to his former home, he scarcely recognized it. He left in despair. The property was then unoccupied for 36 years while it was held by the State of Connecticut. Over the following decades, the other homes along that section of the boundline highway were abandoned and the road gradually became impassable. The forest reclaimed what had been the road. That made the finding of the Gilkey place for future historians a bit more difficult. The closest road was now about one-quarter mile away. In between, there was a dense forest with few markers.

There were some locals that could still find their way to the old Gilkey place and guide those who were unfamiliar with the location. Such was the case when Charles S. Miller, the author of *Peter Gilkey: A Connecticut Counterfeiter*, looked for the Gilkey place on June 18, 1905. He had no luck. On another occasion, September 22, 1908, he was still not successful. But as Miller was leaving the area, he encountered a man named George Cass who knew exactly where it was. Mr. Cass took him right to the spot. From that day on, Mr. Miller acted as a tour guide to his fellow historians who wanted to see the Gilkey place. This practice continued for decades. These facts were detailed in Mr. Miller's daily pocket diary, which he faithfully kept from 1876-1943.

In 1819, Elisha Platt purchased the ten-acre former Gilkey property from the State of Connecticut. There is no indication that Mr. Platt or any subsequent landowners made any improvements to the site. Because the lot became landlocked, access became more difficult. The adjoining highway was referred to as the old abandoned Baldwin Road on maps from the twentieth century. Peter Gilkey Road currently refers to the active portion of the road, which begins a one-half mile south of the Gilkey location.

Eventually, the Gilkey property was consolidated with other adjacent

Major Charles S. Miller greets Mrs. M. E. Pierpont on February 15, 1942. His uniform represents his involvement in the Mattatuck Drum Band, founded in 1767. Mr. Miller was a respected historian from Waterbury but knew a great deal about Prospect. This included the people and their homes, both past and present. He collaborated with historians in Prospect, such as Ruth Hotchkiss and Nellie Cowdell.

Photo: WikiTree

land in the hope of creating an industrial park. The close proximity to Waterbury, an interstate highway, and all the required utilities made that a realistic possibility. That goal never came to pass, but another opportunity emerged at the start of the 21st century.

Archaeological Survey
The ability to find the Gilkey place became much easier within the last two decades because of an unlikely turn of events. When home building contractor Toll Brothers, Inc. decided to construct a major condominium complex called Prospect Commons, Connecticut required them to conduct an archaeological survey of the 177-acre property. The purpose was to determine if there were any historically significant elements. This was completed on September 30, 2005, by American Cultural Specialists, LLC of Seymour, CT. Their investigation looked for Native American sites as well as any Colonial sites.

Their findings indicated there were a number of Native American remnants such as arrow/knife point stones, dated back to 3000-2000 BC. But these were considered typical for almost any land within the United States. They determined this area in Prospect was used as a hunting ground and not an area where any Native American permanent settlements took place. So there was no restriction placed on the Toll development in the Native American category.

As for Colonial structures, the survey designated two areas that needed to remain undeveloped and preserved by Toll Brothers. One was the Abel Austin farmhouse property (from the late 1700s), which contained a cellar hole and the remains of other outbuildings. There were also zigzag stone walls unique to that period, which should be preserved.

The other was the Tuttle/Baldwin et al. residence, which was known to exist in 1811. The author believes the et al. (and other) references would include the Peter Gilkey place, which dates back to 1782. The distance from and location along the boundline highway matched this site. The survey indicated this area also had a well and outbuildings. Because the well was left open and was quite deep, Toll Brothers was directed to fill it with sand as a safety measure.

In a 1954 Waterbury Sunday Republican article, Raymond H. Miller described the Gilkey site as "faintly discernible in the woods." That

Abel Austin farmhouse zig-zag stone wall in Prospect.
Photo: John R. Guevin, 2024

seemed to match how it appears today. His father, Charles S. Miller, wrote in his pocket diary, "The next cellar place north of the Gilkey place where stands a large pine tree known as the Baldwin Place . . .

Daniel Baldwin settled in 1798. It was later occupied by his son Isaac."

Toll Brothers was required to keep those two areas undisturbed, which they did. It is fortunate that Peter Gilkey's place will now be preserved for future generations to understand and learn. The Toll Brothers Prospect Commons was later renamed Regency at Prospect.

Prospect site believed to be the Peter Gilkey place. Looters destroyed the walls of the double basement in search of Spanish dollars.   Photo: John R. Guevin, 2024

FOURTEEN

Conclusions

Now that a more complete story of Peter Gilkey has been revealed, the reader can review those questions that were raised in the introduction. First, why did he get into counterfeiting? The joke answer was to make money. That may be true in this sense—Peter Gilkey may have seen it as a quicker path to prosperity than being a cobbler like his father. He may have rationalized that others were doing things to become prosperous that were not legal. So why not him?

Chiseling and Cheating

According to Raymond H. Miller, son of Charles S. Miller, the demand for hard money was very great in Colonial days. One trick was to chisel small pieces off silver and gold coins. When enough pieces were collected, they were melted down and sold to a silver or goldsmith.

The more sinister practice was to actually make counterfeit coins. The lure of riches or the need for necessities drove otherwise respectable people into this crime.

This attitude may be even more common today. So much in the world around us is fake. It is hard to know what is real. Counterfeits are everywhere. The rip-off watches, pocketbooks, and designer clothes. The list goes on. While counterfeiters in Gilkey's day were strongly vilified, that may not be the case today.

There is a marker sign prominently displayed on the Prospect Green. The first notation listed on the back is: Peter Gilkey, counterfeiter. When people read this, they might snicker. Would his name be so prominently listed if he were a murderer?

Risk Factor
Another answer to the *why* question may be found in Gilkey's life of adventure and risk. This began with his journey to America, filled with perils and uncertainty. Then there was his military career, that spanned two wars. No doubt, some people enjoyed living on the edge. Peter Gilkey demonstrated that he was a risk taker. It is possible he dreamed of a career that involved risk.

Knowledge of Crime
It seemed obvious that he knew what he did was against the law. The extensive measures he took to avoid detection proved that. But did he reveal his plans about counterfeiting to his father? There is evidence that he did not want his father to know. Why did he wait until his father died to put his plan into action?

Counterfeiting Grade
There was little doubt that Gilkey was very skilled at his craft. He was obsessed with making a quality product—even if it was counterfeit. He was also very careful to distance himself from the distribution of

the coins. His argument was that he never used the coins himself. Others did that.

Mistakes Made
But was he a great counterfeiter? The evidence suggested he was not. The best criminals are said to be the ones that don't get caught. They lived out their lives with the appearance of being law-abiding citizens. Their crimes were never uncovered.

Here is one example of where he went wrong. He thought that a rural, remote site would be the best place for his operation. In reality, maybe a loft operation in the heart of a busy city would have been better. In a small town, everyone knew everyone. They knew what others were doing. Secrets were hard to keep. In a city, people were less concerned with, or didn't even know, their neighbors. It would have been easier to keep a counterfeiting operation secret in a city.

There might be another flaw in his plans. Did he have too many partners? It seemed that if he had fewer people involved, he could have kept the operation under wraps for a longer time.

A Better Choice?
Mr. Miller spoke about the quality of Peter Gilkey's coin metal. This confirmed how knowledgeable Gilkey was about his craft. You might go so far as to say he was a genius. Why did he not apply his skills to a legal trade that was in high demand rather than an illegal one like counterfeiting? That question could be asked of many criminals who populated our prisons in the past and those in the present as well.

According to an aged metallurgist, about 1830, Capt. William Mix, who manufactured cast pewter spoons in Rag Hollow [in Prospect], procured by some means the formula that Peter Gilkey used in mixing the metal for his counterfeit dollars. His spoons were greatly improved, as were those manufactured by Titus Mix at Brooksvale in Cheshire. They stamped the spoons with Britannia, a rare metal in those days, in Prospect. It is very seldom that any of Mr. Mix's white metal spoons are to be found now. First German silver replaced the market for pewter and Britannia spoons. Then the local people used the spoons for soldering tinware, a common practice at the time. First the broken and injured spoons were used, bringing about the discovery of the excellent solder they made, and as they were fast going out of use, spoons and ladles of every description were used until now scarcely any remain.

Charles S. Miller

The Victims
Who were the victims of this counterfeiting operation? One example would be anyone who received some of his coins in trade, but then that person was unable to use them because it was determined they were fake. It is less clear about people who exchanged their coins without knowledge or detection of their counterfeit status.

Peter Gilkey may have seen himself as a victim. He may have thought the punishment for his crime was greater than the crime itself. He lost his home, land, and all his resources, plus he went to prison. Peter might have asked, "Was my sentence just?" That could be debated. It is safe to say that when the state sent Susannah and her children to prison, they became victims. There is no doubt about that.

The Heroes
The author pointed out three people that could be considered heroes in chapter eight. The hunter who heard something and said something. Then there was Amias, with his acute perceptions, that solved the mystery. Finally, there was the sheriff, who was not afraid to include a "different" type of person in his investigation. Did the reader find any other heroes in this book?

The Gilkey Children and Their Families
It was earlier mentioned that Peter and Susannah had boys William (~1780-?) and Gary (1782-1854). William and Gary endured the hard-

ships of the Gaol at Hartford as a toddler and an infant respectively. They had a third son, Riley (1784-1834) born on August 8, 1784. He was most likely conceived in that jail. He was born either there or shortly after the Gilkey family was released.

It is now known that Gary and Riley became adults and both relocated to the same area of north-central New York State. They married and had children. Their families settled in a cluster of small towns named Genoa, Locke, Dryden, and Venice. This area was about 275 miles from their parents' home in Connecticut.

Gary Gilkey married Hannah Taylor (1785-1817) about 1809. They had four daughters: Sarah (1810-1890), Nancy (1811-1849), Sylvia (1814-1880), and Hannah (1815-1866). After his first wife died in 1817, he married Joanna Harris (1791-1884) about 1818. They had three daughters and one son: Sophia (1819-1839), Mary (1822-1858), John C. (1825-1845), and Harriet (1827-1860).

Riley Gilkey married (unknown) Taylor Gilkey and they had two children, Orren Taylor (1812-1879) and Charlotte (1816-1816) who died as an infant.

Records with details about Peter and Susannah's son, William, have not been found. He may have died an early death and could have been the child his father described as *being very weakly & never likely to recover* when he was a prisoner at the Gaol at Hartford. Records about the other son and one daughter reported on the U.S. 1790 Census have not surfaced thus far.

The Next Generation
Riley Gilkey's son Orren married Lydia Ann Baker (1816-1878) in 1834. They had seven children born in New York: James Riley (1835-1899), Samuel G. (1837-1921), Francis Asbury "Frank" (1840-1898), Sarah Esther [Tribe] (1845-1896), Orren Alphonse (1848-1861), Lydia Ann [LaBar] (1853-1915) and Charles E. "Charley" (1859-1860).

There is no doubt that information about the Gilkey family genealogy will expand even more in the future from what is detailed here. Gilkey, which was once a rare name in Connecticut and in America in general, is now much more common.

In an Amazon review of the author's book *View from the Top: the story of Prospect, Connecticut*, Chuck Gilkey wrote: *My 8th great-grandfather (a notorious counterfeiter, and revolutionary war soldier) is honored on a historical marker with other notable citizens, many of who have humorous and informative biographies in this book.* Therefore, if your surname is Gilkey (or maybe Tribe or LaBar), you might want to do a bit of research to see if you are related to the infamous Peter Gilkey.

Lessons Learned?
In the end, did Peter Gilkey learn a lesson? Or would he have done it all over again—only smarter the next time?

His return to the cobbler trade would seem to indicate he had gone straight. But after serving his term in prison, where did he get the money to, pay off his fine plus buy his Waterbury home and the lease on his cobbler shop? That raised a red flag for many people. Were the stories about his hidden treasures true? Did all of those fortune seekers who raided his property miss some or all of his hiding places?

This book began with a quest for answers to questions about the life of Peter Gilkey. Now that his story has been told, there seem to be more questions to answer than when the book started. Maybe that's a good thing. History is full of examples where new knowledge answers old questions, but it requires more investigation to answer the uncertainty these revelations create. Like genealogy, the study of history evolves and is seldom settled.

Chronology

1725	Peter Gilkey, Sr. was born in County Donegal, Ireland.
1745	Peter Gilkey, Jr. was born in Ireland.
~ 1750	The Gilkey family moved to America.
1762	Peter Gilkey served in the Colonial Connecticut Expedition for King George III in the French and Indian War in Cuba. He stayed there for an extra year after his term of service ended. He then moved back to Connecticut.
1768	Peter Gilkey married Susannah (1746-?).
1776	Peter Gilkey served in the Connecticut Militia during the American Revolutionary War.
1780	Peter Gilkey, Sr. died in Cheshire.
~ 1780	A son, William Gilkey (~1780-?), was born to Peter and Susannah.
July 5, 1780	Susannah Gilkey purchased land in Cheshire for £6, 3 shillings from Ashel Andrews and Stephen Bunnel.
Feb 25, 1781	Peter and Susannah sold the Cheshire property for £15 to David Morgan.
Oct 31, 1782	A son, Cary Gilkey (1782-1854), was born to Peter and Susannah.
Feb. 18, 1783	Peter Gilkey received a two-year sentence to New-Gate prison plus a fine for counterfeiting. He began serving time at Gaol at Hartford. His wife and children accompanied him because he could not support them.

1783	State of Connecticut seized Gilkey's 10-acre property.
1784	Peter Gilkey was released early from Gaol at Hartford along with his family.
Aug 8, 1784	A son, Riley Gilkey (1782-1834), was born to Peter and Susannah.
Jan. 22, 1785	Peter Gilkey purchased a homestead in East Farms, Waterbury, and leased a cobbler shop.
1785	Peter Gilkey's petition for relief from the counterfeiting fine (because of poverty and a useless hand) was not granted.
Aug 1790	The first U.S. Census revealed Peter Gilkey lived in Cheshire with his wife, four sons under 16, and one daughter.
1818	Peter Gilkey died at age 72-73 and was buried in Waterbury, Connecticut.
1819	Elisha Platt purchased the former Gilkey property from the State of Connecticut.
1827	Prospect was incorporated which included Gilkey property.
2005	Gilkey property given preservation status.

Appendix

Cheshire Land Records
Purchase
Vol. 1, P. 8. 5 July 1780

"Know ye that Asahel Andrews of Cheshire, Administrator on the Estate of Stephen Bunnel of Wallingford Deceased, which Estate is insolvent, sells for £6. 3 shillings, to Susanna Gilkey, wife to Peter Gilkey of Cheshire, a small slip of land with dwelling house on the same, with incumbrance of a widow's dower, being about seven rods. Witnesses: Abijah Hull, Samuel Beach."

Sale
Vol. 1, P. 62. 25 February 1781

"Know ye that we Peter Gilkey and Susannah Gilkey, wife of Peter, Both of Cheshire, County of New Haven, State of Connecticut for the consideration of fifteen pounds, lawful money received, to our full satisfaction of Daniel Morgan, Do Give, Bargain, Sell, and Confirm unto the said Daniel Morgan, One certain piece of land bounds east on highway, south on land belonging to Joseph Morgan north and west on land belonging to the heirs of Stephen Bunnel and others. Being a piece of ground with a dwelling house standing thereon. Being the same that Stephen Bunnel late deceased occupied before his death. Dated Feb. 25th 1781. Peter Gilkey, Susannah Gilkey."

Waterbury Land Records
Purchase
12 February 1782

"Know ye that I Ellas Hotchkiss of New Haven, for the consideration of Eighteen Pounds Lawful Money received to my full satisfaction of Peter Gilkey of Waterbury. Do sell etc. One certain piece of land situated in the town of Waterbury. Laid out in the name of Moses Moss, it being ten acres, bounded east on Cheshire line, north on Charles Hall and south on Jonathan Hall, and to run forty-four rods on Cheshire line, and extend that width till it makes Ten Acres. February 12, 1782. Ellas Hotchkiss."

Purchase
22 January 1785

"Know ye that I John Miller of Waterbury County of New Haven, and State of Connecticut, for the consideration of Twenty Five Pounds Lawful Money Received to my full satisfaction of Peter Gilkey, do Bargain Sell and Confirm, unto the said Peter Gilkey. Thirty Eight rods of land situated in the First Society of Waterbury with a dwelling house standing there on. "Butted and Bounded as follows. Beginning at the parting of two roads from Waterbury to Wallingford and Farmington, then running northeast twelve Rods to a heap of stones, then southeast Four Rods to a heap of stones, then northwest to the first corner. Butting southwardly on the Cheshire Road, westerly on the Farmington Road, north and east on William Munson's land. To have and to hold etc. Dated January 22, A. D. 1785. his John x Miller mark"

Purchase
22 January 1785

"Know all men by these present that I John Miller of Waterbury, in the County of New Haven, and State of Connecticut. For the Consideration of Five Pounds, received to my full satisfaction of Peter Gilkey of said Waterbury, have leased, and by these presents do lease unto him the said Peter Gilkey a certain piece of land situated in said Waterbury for the full term of Nine Hundred and Ninety-Five years with a Shoemaker's Shop standing thereon. Said land is Butted and bounded as follows, northwardly and eastwardly on Highways, and extends six feet west from the northwest corner of said Shop and six feet west from the southwest corner of said Shop. Then running southwardly to Mr. Nathaniel Hoadly's land, And Butts south on Hoadly's land and west on land belonging to Reuben Benham's heirs. Dated January 22, A. D. 1785. his John x Miller mark"

Purchase
Former Gilkey Property from State of Connecticut
16 March 1819

"Know all men by these presents that I Isaac Spencer as Treasurer of the State on Connecticut. For divers good causes there unto moving. Especially for the sum of Thirty-five dollars. Received to my full satisfaction of Elisha Platt. Have Remised, Released and forever quit-claimed unto the said Elisha Platt and to his heirs and assignees forever, all such right and title as the said State of Connecticut have or bought in and one certain piece of land lying and being situated in the town of Waterbury in said State of Connecticut, and is bounded as follows, via. On the east by highway dividing the towns of Waterbury and Cheshire on the south by land of said Elisha Platt. On the west by lands of Eldad Hotchkiss. On the north by Daniel Baldwin's land. Containing about three acres, be the same more or less. To have and to hold the said premises; unto him the Elisha Platt his heirs and assignees forever. So that neither the State of Connecticut or any other person, in their name and behoof shall or will here after claim or demand any right or title to the premises or any part thereof, but they and any of them, shall by these presents be excluded and forever debarred.

"In witness whereof, I have here unto set my hand and seal. This sixteenth day of March in the year of our Lord 1819. Signed sealed and delivered In the presence of Isaac Spenser (L. L.), George Stanley, Elisha Colt

"Hartford, County of Hartford, March 16, 1819. Personally appeared Isaac Spenser, Signer and sealer of the foregoing Instrument and Acknowledged the same before me to be his free-act and deed.

Elisha Colt. Justice of Peace."

County of New Haven Court Records
Revolutionary War Service

"New Haven County Court, Holden at New Haven, State of Connecticut.
"Peter Gilkey, a soldier of Wallingford, living in the limits of the 15 Company, 10th Regiment. Being drilled on the 26th day of May last, to fill up the Continental Army, by Jesse Moss, Captain of said Company, and refusing to, was summoned to this Court to answer as per Writ, dated Sept. 10, 1777: said Gilkey appearing pleaded Not Guilty. This Court on Consideration are of the opinion. He is not Guilty. It is there upon Considered that he be released on paying last tax at L 1: 19. 9. Ex. Granted Mar. 26, 1778."

County of New Haven Court Records
Found Guilty and Sentenced

"Sheriff or his Deputy, Greetings. Whereas Peter Gilkey of Waterbury in the County of New Haven, on the last Tuesday of February 1783 before the Superior Court held at New Haven, was found Guilty of making instruments for forging and Counterfeiting Spanish Dollars, where of said Court under Judgment against the said Peter that he be committed to the Common Gaol in Hartford, there to remain until the New-Gate Prison shall be repaired and fit to receive Prisoners and then be committed to New-Gate Prison. His imprisonment on the whole to be full two years, and that he pay a fine to and for the use of this State the sum of Thirty Pounds Lawful money, and pay the costs of suit Taxed at L.17"18"3 Lawful money as appears of record, where of Execution remains to be done.

Fined and Sent to Prison

"These are therefore in the Name of the Government and Company of the State of Connecticut to Command you to take the body of said Peter Gilkey, and him commit unto the keeper of the Gaol in Hartford within the prison, who is hereby to receive him and safely keep until the New-Gate Prison shall be repaired, and the Sheriff of Hartford County is commanded to commit him to said New-Gate Prison, and of the goods, chattels, or lands of the said Peter, you are to collect the sum of Thirty Pounds Lawful money. The Lawful Costs which is L. 17"18"3 Lawful money out of his goods, chattels, or lands, and the same being disposed of, or appraised as the law directs, pay and satisfy the Treasurer of this State, for the time being with your own fees. Here of fail not, but make due return within sixty days. Dated at New Haven February 18, 1783 A.D. William Pitkin Clerk, P. I."

Property Seized and Appraised

"New Haven County, Waterbury, 5 day of March 1783 with this Writ I repaired to the usual abode of the defendant and there make demand of money, or Chattels to satisfy the same and my fees. But none were shown unto me, there at the Special Direction of the Superior Court. I levied it on a lot of land in said Waterbury containing ten acres, bounded north on Charles Hull, east on Cheshire line, south on Jonathan Hall, and to run north forty-four Rods on Cheshire line and to extend west that width till it makes ten Acres, with a dwelling house there on standing.

"The Creditors appointed Mr. Michael Bronson to appraise said land, and the Defendants refusing to appoint. I applied to Mr. Jonathan Baldwin the nearest Justice of the Peace for said County who did appoint Messrs. William Levenworth, and Stephen Ives who being duly sworn, and having carefully viewed the premises, did appraise the same at Forty-five Pounds Lawful Money. The Debt and Costs together with the costs of appraising being L. 56 Lawful Money, much more than of said land and house, is hereby set off with all the appearances to the state in part payment for this execution. A. Feste Samuel Thatcher, Sheriff

We the subscribers Chosen, appointed as above, did appraise said land and House above described at L. 35 Lawful money. Stephen Ives

Appraisers Michael Bronson Wm. Levenworth"

Peter Gilkey Set Free

Upon the Memorial of Peter Gilkey of Waterbury in New Haven County showing to this Assembly that in February last he was convicted before Honorable Superior Court holden at New Haven in said county for counterfeiting money and sentenced to two years imprisonment in NewGate & praying for interposition of the clemency and grace of this Assemble. *Resolved by this Assembly* that the said Peter Gilkey be discharged from any further imprisonment in virtue of said conviction and the Keeper of the Gaol at Hartford is hereby directed to liberate the said Gilkey accordingly.

Public Records of Connecticut

Work Record Pocket Diaries of Charles Somers Miller
Peter Gilkey

06/18/1905 (Sunday)
Went with B.F. Howland out on the old town bound looking after the Peter Gilkey cellar.

09\22\1908 (Sunday)
This day Frank and I went out on the old boundary road that formerly divided Waterbury from Wallingford and later from Cheshire and still divides Waterbury from Cheshire from the Meriden Road south to the Prospect town line but now continues in a strait southerly direction to Straitsville.
We were in search of the old Peter Gilkey place cellar and after searching a long time were returning home when we met George Cass in the woods and he went back and showed me. It is in the town of Prospect on the west side of the old highway about a good quarter of a mile north of where the present traveled road turns east from it near the house owned by William Purdy. The next cellar place north of the Gilkey place where stands a large pine tree known as the Baldwin Place . . .

03\12\1911 (Sunday)
Mrs. Noble came this evening after service and I gave her all the information that I had concerning Peter Gilkey the man who counterfeited Spanish Milled dollars at his house in Prospect in 1783 and was sent to New-Gate Prison.

05\10\1936 (Sunday)
In the afternoon John Heinion and I went to the South end of the Scott road and explores it clear up through. We also went over on the old Bound Line

road and visited the site of the Old Daniel Baldwin and Peter Gilkey places.
10\16\1938 (Sunday)
This afternoon I went to Mr. Wilsons on the Summit Road in Prospect, where we had supper. While there we visited the old Daniel Baldwin place and the place where Peter Gilkey the counterfeiter lived when he was arrested in 1783.
04/08/1940 (Monday)
This evening I went out to Ralph Pierpont's and read a paper on Peter Gilkey, the Revolutionary Counterfeiter.

Nellie Cowdell Typing

05\17\1932 (Tuesday)
This morning I took some work to Miss Cowdell in Prospect to have typewritten.
10\10\1932 (Monday)
This morning I went to Mr. Cowdell's in Prospect and left some typing to be done.
07\28\1933 (Friday)
I then went to Prospect and paid Nellie Cowdell 1.00 for typewriting over paid .25...

CT Crimes and Misdemeanors Series 1
Peter Gilkey Petition Summaries

Gilkey, Peter, Waterbury, counterfeiting. Physician's certificate that he is liable to lose the use of one of his hands & health is much impaired, Jan. 1783 VI: 213

Gilkey, Peter, Petition showing sentence to two years in Newgate & forfeiture of all his estate for counterfeiting. As the only evidence was some tools found in his house & as he never passed bills he asks pardon, granted May 1783 VI: 215,216

Gilkey, Peter, Waterbury, sentenced to 2 years at Newgate for having tools in his possession & estate forfeited. Petition for pardon on account of poor health, granted May 1783 V1: 213-216

Gilkey, Peter, Letter asking attorney to petition for his release or at least for change to New Haven Gaol, Oct.1783 VI: 214

Gilkey, Peter, Physicians' certificates of his hand being useless 1784 V1: 281,282

Gilkey, Peter, Petition showing imprisonment & fine of £30 for counterfeiting & asking release from fine on account of poverty & useless hand, Oct. 1785 VI: 280

Gilkey, Peter, petition for relief from fine on account of poverty & useless hand, 1785 VI: 280-282

Accomplices' Petitions

Perkins, William, Cheshire, sentenced for making forge for Peter Gilkey & petition for liberty granted on giving bond for good behavior & payment of costs, Oct.1783 VI: 229,230

Tyler, Abraham, Waterbury, taxed for costs of trial for altering bill in which he was acquitted. Petition for discharge from same neg. May 1771 V: 342

Tyler, Abraham sentenced for assisting Peter Gilkey in making forge. Liberty allowed on payment of costs & giving £200 bond for good behavior, Oct.1783 VI: 231,232

Peter Gilkey Petition Details

"The Memorial of Peter Gilkey of Waterbury to the General Assembly humbly sheweth: That in Feby last he was convicted before the honble Sup^r Court for Counterfeiting money & Sentinced to two years imprisonment in Newgate beside the forfeiture of all his Estate—that the only Evidence against him was some Tools or Instruments" (he neglects to mention the die) found in his house, supposed (to be used in) Counterfeiting, that upon this Ground it was presumed he had been concerned in making base money —he freely confesseth with Shame & remorse before Your Honors, that he was reduced to this wicked scheme & was about to put it into Execution but never in fact did do it—for these Evil intentions he acknowledges the just desert of punishment, but humbly begs under his present distrest Circomstances, that your Honor^g would be satisfied with the forfeiture of his Estate & the Imprisonment he hath suffered hitherto & solomly promises never more to offend. He hath a wife & children now with him in Prison, feeling most Sensibly the effects of his folly—they are destitute & distrest and have nothing—the memorialist is also wounded in one of his hands and fears it will be lost intirely & is sick & worn down with his unhappy Situation— wherefore he most Earnestly begs your Honors Graciously to forgive the remainder of his Imprisonment & suffer him to go home with his poor Family & begin the world anew & live in Peace with all men, which by God's Grace, he determines to Doe, & he as in Duty bound will ever pray. Dated at the Gaol, May 1783."

"Upon the Memorial of Peter Gilkey of Waterbury in New Haven County Shewing to his Assembly that in February last he was Convicted before the Honble Court holden in New Haven in said County for Counterfeiting Money and Sentenced to two Years Imprisonment in Newgate & Praying for the Interposition or the Clemency and Grace of this Assembly. Resolved by this Assembly that the said Peter Gilkey be discharged from any further Imprisonment in Virtue of said Conviction and the Keeper of the Gaol at Hartford is hereby to liberate the said Gilkey accordingly"

"Memorial of Peter Gilkey of Waterbury humbly Sheweth —That in Feb[y] 1783 before the Sup[r] Court at New Haven he was sentenced to two years Imprisonment, to pay a fine of 30 pounds Cost 19 pounds upon suspicion of being about to be concerned in the counterfeit scheme—that your Honors have Graciously pleased to remit a part of the Imprisonment the Memorial[st] begs leave further to represent that while he was in Jail he most unfortunately, by an accident (had) a wound in his left hand & wrist, so that he hath almost wholly lost the intire use of it—that he hath a wife & children to support, one of his children being very weakly & never like to recover, & is very chargeable & helpless which greatly adds to the poverty & Distress of the Meml[st]. That his small house & Ten acres of indifferent Land is all he has in the world and this has been taken from him to satisfy the afore[sd] Fine and Cost—The Meml[st] earnestly entreats Your Honors Mercifully to forgive him the said Fine & he will struggle to secure the Cost—otherwise he & his Family must fall a Charge upon the public—or relieve him in some way & save him & his Family from utter Ruin—his Crime was intentional, if anything, it never proceeded to overt act, as their Honors the Judges can Inform & . . . A. Dom.1784"

Bibliography

Cheshire Historical Society, records.
Connecticut From the Best Authorities, Map 1796, Cheshire Library.
Connecticut's Old Newgate Prison, 1989, Edited by Dorothy A. DeBisschop and Carol Stone.
Connecticut, US, Town Birth Records, Pre-1870, Barbour Collection.
Crimes and Misdemeanors, 1st Series, 1774-1788, CT State Library.
CT Genealogical Database Individual, Sunshine.Rahul.net.
FamilySearch.org.
FindaGrave.com
Geni.com/People.
Gilkey Genealogy Letters, 1947, George L. Gilkey.
Heads of Families at the First Census of the United States Taken in the Year 1790, Bureau of the Census.
Land Records, Cheshire, Connecticut, Town Clerk.
Land Records, Milford, Connecticut, City Clerk.
Land Records, Prospect, Connecticut, Town Clerk.
Land Records, Wallingford, Connecticut, Town Clerk.
Land Records, Waterbury, Connecticut, City Clerk.
Naugatuck Daily News, Newspaper Article 1952.
Newgate: From Copper Mine to State Prison, 1998, William G. Domonell.
New Haven County, Connecticut Court Records 1665-1855, 1936, Hartford Connecticut State Library.
Northern Ireland - Plantations, Conflict, Union, Britannica.com.
OurFamilyTree.org.
Passenger Ships from Ireland to America 1732-1749, GenealogyBranches.com.
Peter Gilkey: A Connecticut Counterfeiter, 1940 manuscript, Charles S. Miller.
Peter Gilkey a Counterfeiter: Some Comments Upon His Life and Evil Deeds, 1962, The Mattatuck Historical Society.
Phase 1 Archaeological Reconnaissance Survey & Phase 2 Intensive Archaeological Survey of the Proposed Prospect Commons Property in Prospect, Connecticut, American Cultural Specialists, LLC.
Prospect Historical Society, records.
Prospect No. 4, Prospect Soldiers 1775-1783, 1976, Nellie Cowdell.
Public Records of Connecticut, 1783, Hartford Connecticut State Library.
US, Revolutionary War Service Records, 1775-1783, The National Archives.
View from the Top: the story of Prospect, Connecticut, 1995, John R. Guevin.
Wikitree.com.
Waterbury Sunday Republican, Newspaper Article, March 7, 1954.
Work Record Pocket Diaries, 1876-1943, Charles S. Miller.

Other Books by the Author

Who's Who Directory for Cheshire, Connecticut

Uncommon Cats: The Who's Who of Cats

More Uncommon Cats!

*View from the Top:
the story of Prospect, Connecticut*

View from
the Top

The author has assisted nearly 100 other authors to have their books published through Biographical Publishing Company since 1991.

Biographical
Publishing
Company

roduct-compliance